GEMINI
May 21–June 20

You
have absolute
control over
just one thing,
your thoughts.

✦ Napoleon Hill ✦

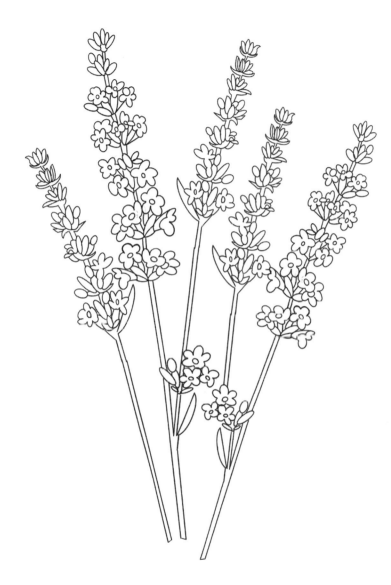

LAVENDER

Gemini

I
AM
READY

♊

spring

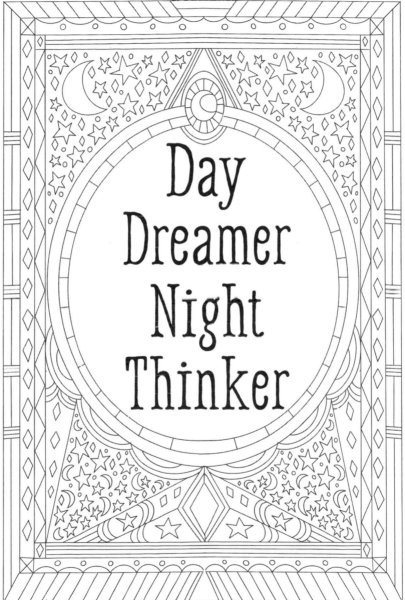

Gemini

Day
Dreamer
Night
Thinker

Creative

Outgoing

CURIOUS

INTELLIGENT

PERCEPTIVE

GEMINI

✧

My dreams are my reality

✦✧✦

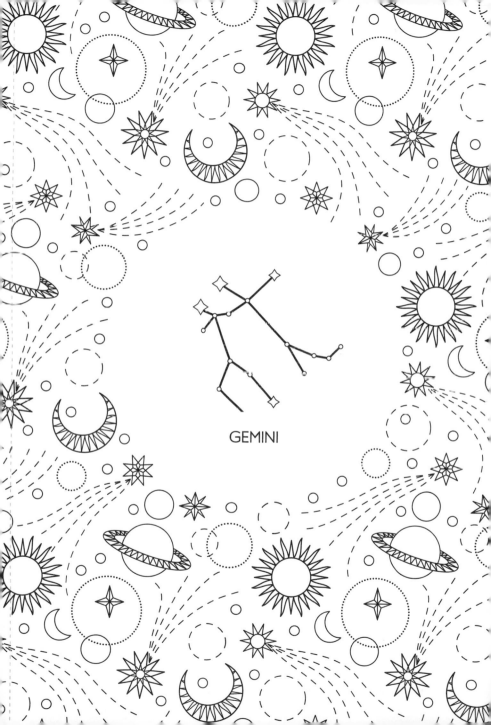

GEMINI

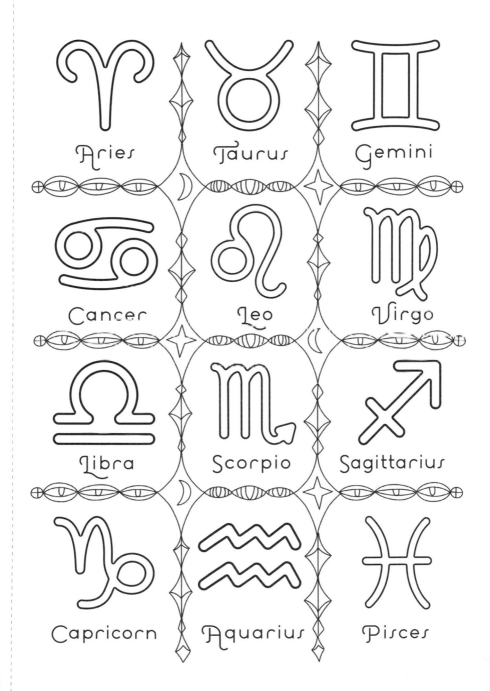

Air Signs

Aquarius

Libra

Gemini

LET THE STARS LEAD THE WAY